A. A. Milne

The Milne family lived in a
small London school, where
Mr Milne was headmaster. There
were two sons, Barry and Ken.
In 1882, a third son was born.
He was named Alan Alexander –
A. A. Milne.

As soon as they were old enough, Alan and his brothers became pupils at their father's school. It was a happy school and everyone thought Mr Milne was a brilliant teacher.

Alan loved school work. His favourite subject was maths. He often did better than his older brothers. He was messy, though, and was always losing things.

When he was eleven, Alan joined his brother Ken at a famous school called Westminster. Alan did so well that he moved up into Ken's class. Ken wasn't jealous – he and Alan were best friends.

They went everywhere together. They even wrote messages to each other in lessons. To make it more fun, they missed out every other word.

But Alan didn't like Westminster. He found it a strict, miserable place and he lost interest in school work. Later he studied at Cambridge University, but he didn't do well in his exams. His father was disappointed in him.

Oh dear... A third class degree for Alan.

Alan had discovered, though, that he loved writing. He and Ken started writing poems together. Soon Alan was writing by himself.

Alan moved to London and
wrote articles and poems for
newspapers and magazines.
At first he didn't make much
money. Often he went to Ken's
house for his meals.

But gradually Alan became more successful. He wrote funny pieces for a famous magazine called *Punch*. People loved them.

In 1913, Alan got married. His wife, Daphne, came from a very rich family.

The next year, the First World War broke out. Alan was a pacifist – he believed that war was wrong. But he still volunteered to be a soldier.

In 1916 he was sent to the Somme, in France. Thousands of men had been killed in a terrible battle there. Alan was lucky. After only a few months, he caught a fever and was sent home.

While he was in the army, Alan
spent all his spare time writing
plays. After the war, people
flocked to the theatres and Alan's
plays did very well. He soon
became famous and earned a
great deal of money.

And he became a father, too. In 1920 Daphne had a baby boy. They called him Christopher Robin.

When Christopher Robin was three, the Milnes went on a trip to Wales with some friends. It was very wet and everyone was miserable. Alan sat in the summerhouse and wrote poems.

One was about Christopher and his nanny. The nanny's name was Olive, but in the poem Alan called her Alice, because he needed a name that rhymed with 'palace'.

Other poems were about things Alan remembered from his own childhood. There was a game that you could play on pavements, called 'Lines and Squares'. You had to avoid treading on the lines.

Alan wrote more poems when
he got back to London. At last
there were enough to make a
whole book. He called the book
When We Were Very Young.

Alan's publishers weren't keen on the idea of a children's book, but they published it anyway. It was a great success – so they asked him to write another.

Alan racked his brains. Daphne suggested a bedtime story that he had already made up for Christopher Robin.

The story was about Christopher, his teddy bear, some bees and a balloon.

Christopher had been given the
teddy for his first birthday. To
start with it was just called Bear.
But when he was about four,
Christopher gave it a new name:
Winnie-the-Pooh.

Christopher had other toys called Eeyore and Piglet. He and Daphne spent hours playing with them. Often Alan watched.

Alan wrote down the bedtime story, as well as some new ones. He wrote about Eeyore and Piglet, and made up two new characters – Rabbit and Owl.

Then Alan and Daphne went to a toy shop to look for some new toys for the stories.

They brought home Kanga and
baby Roo.

The pictures for Alan's poems had been drawn by an artist called Ernest Shepard. Now Ernest visited the Milnes' house and drew Christopher Robin, Piglet, Eeyore, Kanga and Roo for the new stories.

Ernest didn't draw Christopher's Winnie-the-Pooh, though. Instead he drew a teddy called Growler, which belonged to his own son.

The Milnes had two houses, one in London and one near Ashdown Forest in Sussex. This was the forest in the Pooh stories. Alan took Ernest to see all the important places there.

Winnie-the-Pooh was published in 1926.

It was an enormous success and thousands of copies were sold straight away.

Next Alan wrote another book of poems, called *Now We Are Six*. He wrote a second book of Pooh stories too, called *The House at Pooh Corner*. For this he bought a new toy character: Tigger.

Look everyone. Here's your new friend, Tigger.

Both new books sold in vast numbers, but Alan didn't want to write any more of them.

No, I've decided. That's my last children's book.

One reason for this was that Christopher Robin had become very famous. Reporters asked Alan about him all the time. Alan was worried.

At first Christopher enjoyed the fame. But later, when he went away to boarding school, he was badly teased. He began to hate the books, and even blamed his father for writing about him.

Alan had mixed feelings about the books, too. His plays weren't popular any more. He didn't like the idea that he would be remembered only for his children's writing.

Meanwhile, his brother Ken had fallen ill. He and Alan were still best friends, and Alan helped support Ken's family when Ken had to give up his job. But in 1929 Ken died, aged 48.

Soon it looked as if there would be another war. Alan campaigned for peace and wrote a book called *Peace With Honour*.

But in 1939 Britain declared war with Germany. Though Alan was against war, he now realised that the German leader, Hitler, had made plans so terrible that fighting was the only way to stop him.

37

Christopher joined the army as an engineer. Alan and Daphne stayed at their house in Sussex, where they looked after children sent away from London. Sometimes enemy planes dropped bombs nearby.

Why do the planes come here?

They're on their way to bomb London.

Even during the war, Alan's four children's books kept on selling. Paper was scarce, and the publishers found it difficult to keep up with the demand.

When the war was over, Christopher's famous toys went on a tour of America. Fans travelled hundreds of miles to see them. Alan's American

publishers were so delighted that
Alan let them keep the toys.
Today they are on display in the
New York Public Library.

Now Alan had so much money
that he didn't have to worry if a
new book didn't sell.

But Alan *did* worry. He wrote a
book of short stories. It wasn't a
success, and he was very sad.

It's not a very good
review, dear.

Alan was also sad because he and Christopher didn't get on very well any more. Christopher had gone to run a bookshop in Devon.

I miss him. I wish he would visit more often.

When he was 70, Alan had a
stroke. It made him partly
paralysed, and he went to live
in a nursing home.

I can still write a letter to
The Times, you know!

Still, every year, more and more people bought his poems and Pooh stories. When he died, aged 74, Alan knew that – against his wishes – he would be remembered as a children's writer after all.

Further facts

A strange name for a bear

Neither Christopher Milne nor his father could quite remember how Winnie-the-Pooh got his name. Winnie was the name of a bear at London Zoo that Christopher had seen, and he had once named a swan 'Pooh', so perhaps he just put the two together.

Billy and Moon

Christopher Robin is a famous name, but when he was little the real

Christopher Milne was known as 'Billy' instead. Later he had another nickname, 'Moon', which was how 'Milne' came out when he first tried to say it.

The real Roo mystery

Pooh, Piglet, Eeyore, Kanga and Tigger are in the New York Public Library, but one toy isn't there: Roo. In the Pooh stories Roo often goes missing, and is always found. But when the real Roo got lost one day near the Milnes' Sussex home, though everyone searched and searched, he was never seen again.

Some important dates in A. A. Milne's lifetime

1882 Alan Alexander Milne is born in London, third son of Maria and John Vine Milne.

1893 Alan becomes a pupil at Westminster School.

1900 Alan starts his studies at Trinity College, Cambridge.

1903 Alan moves to London, wanting to be a writer.

1913 Now a successful writer, Alan marries Dorothy de Selincourt, known as 'Daphne'.

1914-18 The First World War. Alan becomes a signals officer and is sent to the Somme. He develops 'trench fever' and returns home three months later.

1920 Christopher Robin Milne is born.

1924-28 Alan's four children's books are published: *When We Were Very Young*, *Winnie-the-Pooh*, *Now We Are Six* and *The House at Pooh Corner*. They are all an enormous success.

1929 Kenneth Milne dies of tuberculosis, aged 48.

1952 Alan has a stroke and is left partly paralysed.

1956 Alan dies, aged 74.